Mastering Time Management: Achieving Success in a Busy World

**Chapter 1: Introduction to Time Management**

Defining Time Management

Time is an invaluable resource that, once spent, cannot be reclaimed. It is the great equalizer – every person on this planet has the same 24 hours in a day. How you choose to use those hours can make all the difference in your life. That's where time management comes into play.

Time Management Defined

Time management is the practice of consciously and purposefully planning, organizing, and controlling your tasks and activities in order to make the most efficient and productive use of your time. It involves setting goals, prioritizing tasks, and allocating specific amounts of time to accomplish them. The ultimate goal of time management is to enhance your effectiveness, reduce stress, and improve your overall quality of life.

In a nutshell, time management is about working smarter, not harder. It's not about squeezing as many tasks as possible into your day but about achieving your goals with less stress and more focus.

The Importance of Effective Time Management

Effective time management is a critical skill for achieving success in all aspects of life. Here's why it's so important:

Boosts Productivity: Properly managed time allows you to accomplish more in less time, leading to increased productivity. Whether at work or in your personal life, this can result in achieving your goals faster.

Reduces Stress: Feeling overwhelmed by a never-ending to-do list is a common source of stress. Effective time management helps you gain control over your tasks, reducing stress and anxiety.

Improves Decision-Making: With a clear sense of your priorities, you can make better decisions about where to invest your time and energy.

Enhances Work-Life Balance: Time management can help you strike a balance between your professional and personal life, ensuring that you have time for the things that matter most to you.

Helps You Achieve Your Goals: Time management is essential for setting and achieving goals. By allocating time to work on specific tasks and projects, you're more likely to make progress toward your objectives.

Increases Self-Discipline: It requires discipline to stick to a schedule and avoid distractions. Effective time management can help you build self-discipline, a valuable trait in personal and professional life.

Enables Continuous Improvement: By regularly assessing your time management practices and making adjustments, you can continually refine your approach and become more efficient over time.

Enhances Professional and Personal Relationships: Having time for friends and family can strengthen your personal relationships. At work, it can improve collaboration and teamwork.

Unlocks More Opportunities: As you become more efficient and accomplish your tasks, you free up time for additional opportunities, be it learning a new skill or pursuing a new hobby.

In this book, we will delve into various time management techniques, strategies, and best practices that you can apply in your daily life. Whether you're a student, a professional, an entrepreneur, or a stay-at-home parent, effective time management is a skill that can transform your life, making it more fulfilling and successful. So, let's begin this journey toward mastering the art of time management, and in the process, unlock your true potential.

**Chapter 2: The Psychology of Time**

Introduction:

Time is a fundamental aspect of our lives, governing our daily routines, decisions, and experiences. In this chapter, we will delve into the psychology of time, exploring how our perception of time affects our behavior and well-being. By understanding your relationship with time, you can gain insights into your habits, improve time management, and ultimately lead a more fulfilling life.

Section 1: The Perceived Nature of Time

1.1 Subjective Time Perception:

Time perception varies among individuals. Some people feel time passing slowly, while others feel it rushing by. We'll explore the factors influencing these subjective experiences.

1.2 The Past, Present, and Future:

We'll examine how people focus on the past, present, and future differently. Understanding your temporal orientation can provide insights into your personality and decision-making.

1.3 Time as a Psychological Construct:

Discuss how time is a mental construct, and how cultural and societal influences shape our perception of time.

Section 2: Identifying Time-Wasting Behaviors

2.1 Procrastination:

Delve into the psychology of procrastination and provide practical strategies for overcoming it.

2.2 Multitasking:

Explore the myth of multitasking, its impact on productivity, and how to shift to more effective single-tasking.

2.3 Perfectionism:

Examine the link between perfectionism and time-wasting, and offer tips on how to strike a balance between quality and efficiency.

2.4 Digital Distractions:

Discuss the role of smartphones, social media, and technology in time-wasting, and provide strategies for managing digital distractions.

2.5 Unproductive Habits:

Identify common unproductive habits that consume your time and energy, such as excessive meetings or lack of prioritization.

Section 3: Strategies for Effective Time Management

3.1 Setting Goals and Priorities:

Teach the importance of setting clear goals and priorities to make
the most of your time.

3.2 Time-Blocking and Scheduling:

Explain time-blocking techniques and the benefits of creating
structured schedules.

3.3 Delegation and Outsourcing:

Discuss the value of delegating tasks and outsourcing when
necessary to free up your time.

3.4 Time Management Tools and Apps:

Introduce various time management tools and apps that can assist
in better time management.

3.5 Mindfulness and Time Awareness:

Explore how mindfulness practices can help improve your time
awareness and decision-making.

Conclusion:

In this chapter, we've explored the psychology of time, identified
common time-wasting behaviors, and discussed strategies for
effective time management. Understanding your relationship with

time and implementing these techniques can lead to a more productive and fulfilling life. In the next chapter, we will delve deeper into the practical applications of these concepts in various aspects of your life.

**Chapter 3: Setting SMART Goals**

Introduction:

Setting goals is a fundamental aspect of personal and professional development. In this chapter, we will explore the concept of SMART goals, which stands for Specific, Measurable, Achievable, Relevant, and Time-bound. By using this framework, you can increase your chances of success and achieve your desired outcomes. We will also discuss effective goal-setting strategies to help you put SMART goals into action.

Section 1: Understanding SMART Goals

1.1 Specific Goals:

Learn the importance of setting clear and specific goals. Understand how specificity helps in defining the desired outcome.

1.2 Measurable Goals:

Discuss the significance of measurable goals, which allow you to track progress and determine when the goal has been achieved.

1.3 Achievable Goals:

Explore the concept of achievable goals, including the role of self-assessment, resources, and realistic expectations.

1.4 Relevant Goals:

Understand the importance of relevance in goal setting and how it ensures that your goals align with your values and long-term objectives.

1.5 Time-Bound Goals:

Discuss the necessity of setting time-bound goals, including the benefits of establishing deadlines and timeframes.

Section 2: Goal-Setting Strategies

2.1 Identifying Your Goals:

Learn how to identify your personal and professional goals, and the role of introspection and self-awareness in this process.

2.2 Prioritization:

Explore techniques for prioritizing your goals and focusing on the most critical ones.

2.3 Breaking Goals into Milestones:

Discuss the benefits of breaking large goals into smaller, achievable milestones, making the overall goal more manageable.

2.4 Creating Action Plans:

Understand the importance of action plans in goal achievement, including setting specific steps and strategies to reach your goals.

2.5 Monitoring and Adjusting Goals:

Explore how to track your progress, identify obstacles, and adjust your goals when necessary to stay on course.

2.6 Motivation and Persistence:

Discuss the role of motivation and persistence in achieving your SMART goals, and strategies for maintaining commitment.

Conclusion:

Setting SMART goals is a powerful tool for achieving your desired outcomes in life. By making your goals Specific, Measurable, Achievable, Relevant, and Time-bound, you create a roadmap for success. In this chapter, we've also discussed effective goal-setting strategies to help you implement SMART goals in various aspects of your life. In the next chapter, we will explore the importance of adaptability and flexibility when working toward your goals.

**Chapter 4: Prioritizing Your Tasks**

Introduction:

Effective task prioritization is a key skill for personal and professional productivity. In this chapter, we will explore two powerful methods for prioritizing tasks: Eisenhower's Urgent-Important Matrix and the 4 D's - Do, Delegate, Defer, Delete. These techniques will help you make informed decisions about how to allocate your time and resources efficiently.

Section 1: Eisenhower's Urgent-Important Matrix

1.1 Understanding the Matrix:

Explain the concept of the Urgent-Important Matrix, which categorizes tasks based on their urgency and importance.

1.2 Quadrant I - Urgent and Important:

Describe tasks in Quadrant I, which require immediate attention and why they are critical.

1.3 Quadrant II - Not Urgent but Important:

Explain the significance of tasks in Quadrant II, which are important for long-term goals but don't have an immediate deadline.

1.4 Quadrant III - Urgent but Not Important:

Discuss tasks in Quadrant III, which may seem urgent but are not directly related to your key goals.

1.5 Quadrant IV - Not Urgent and Not Important:

Explain why tasks in Quadrant IV should be minimized or eliminated from your to-do list.

Section 2: The 4 D's - Do, Delegate, Defer, Delete

2.1 The "Do" Strategy:

Discuss when and how to tackle tasks in Quadrants I and II by taking immediate action.

2.2 The "Delegate" Strategy:

Explain how to delegate tasks to others when they fall within their expertise or responsibilities.

2.3 The "Defer" Strategy:

Explore the concept of deferring tasks in Quadrants I and II, making a conscious choice to address them later.

2.4 The "Delete" Strategy:

Discuss when and why it's beneficial to eliminate tasks from your to-do list, especially those in Quadrants III and IV.

Section 3: Implementing Task Prioritization

3.1 Daily Task Management:

Provide guidance on how to apply both the Urgent-Important Matrix and the 4 D's to your daily task management.

3.2 Time Management and Efficiency:

Explain how these prioritization techniques can lead to improved time management and increased efficiency.

3.3 Stress Reduction:

Discuss how effective task prioritization can reduce stress by focusing on the most critical and meaningful tasks.

3.4 Long-Term Goal Achievement:

Highlight how consistently prioritizing tasks can lead to the achievement of long-term personal and professional goals.

Conclusion:

Prioritizing your tasks using methods like Eisenhower's Urgent-Important Matrix and the 4 D's can greatly enhance your productivity and time management skills. By categorizing and handling tasks based on their urgency and importance, you'll be better equipped to focus on what truly matters and achieve your goals. In the next chapter, we will explore strategies for time management and goal tracking to further support your task prioritization efforts.

**Chapter 5: Creating a To-Do List**

Introduction:

A well-structured to-do list is a powerful tool for enhancing productivity and staying organized. In this chapter, we will explore the different types of to-do lists and provide guidance on how to effectively structure your daily to-do list. By mastering the art of creating and managing to-do lists, you can take control of your tasks and achieve your goals more efficiently.

Section 1: Different Types of To-Do Lists

1.1 Traditional To-Do Lists:

Explain the basic concept of a traditional to-do list, where tasks are listed in a linear format, and discuss their advantages and limitations.

1.2 Electronic To-Do Lists:

Explore the use of digital tools and apps for creating to-do lists, and how they can provide added functionality and accessibility.

1.3 Project-Based To-Do Lists:

Discuss project-based to-do lists, which are structured around specific projects or goals, helping you focus on tasks related to a particular objective.

1.4 Time-Blocking To-Do Lists:

Explain time-blocking to-do lists, which allocate specific time slots to tasks and activities, providing a structured daily schedule.

1.5 Goal-Oriented To-Do Lists:

Explore how goal-oriented to-do lists align with long-term objectives, emphasizing tasks that contribute to your overarching goals.

Section 2: How to Structure Your Daily To-Do List

2.1 Prioritization:

Discuss the importance of prioritizing tasks on your daily to-do list and offer techniques for deciding what tasks should take precedence.

2.2 Setting Realistic Goals:

Explain the significance of setting achievable and realistic goals on your to-do list to avoid feeling overwhelmed.

2.3 Time Management:

Provide guidance on managing your time effectively by allocating appropriate time slots to each task on your list.

2.4 Breaking Down Tasks:

Discuss the benefits of breaking down larger tasks into smaller, more manageable subtasks on your to-do list.

2.5 Review and Reflection:

Highlight the importance of reviewing and reflecting on your daily to-do list to make adjustments and improve future planning.

Section 3: Tips and Tools for To-Do List Success

3.1 Use of Technology:

Explore how technology and productivity apps can enhance your to-do list management.

3.2 Consistency and Routine:

Discuss the advantages of incorporating your to-do list into your daily routine for maximum efficiency.

3.3 Flexibility:

Explain how to balance structure and flexibility on your to-do list to accommodate unexpected events and changes.

Conclusion:

Creating and managing a to-do list that aligns with your goals and daily needs is a valuable skill for boosting productivity. Whether you prefer traditional, electronic, project-based, time-blocking, or goal-oriented lists, the key is to structure your to-do list effectively. By mastering these techniques and incorporating them into your daily routine, you can take control of your tasks and accomplish more with less stress. In

the next chapter, we will explore techniques for effective time
management and overcoming common time-related challenges.

**Chapter 6: Time Tracking and Analysis**

Introduction:

Effective time management requires an understanding of how you currently spend your time. In this chapter, we will explore the practice of keeping a time log and how to analyze your time usage. By tracking and analyzing your time, you can identify areas for improvement, make informed decisions, and optimize your daily routines.

Section 1: Keeping a Time Log

1.1 What is a Time Log?

Define a time log as a record of how you allocate your time throughout the day, usually broken down into intervals.

1.2 The Importance of Time Logging:

Explain why keeping a time log is valuable for gaining insight into your daily habits and identifying inefficiencies.

1.3 Types of Time Logs:

Discuss different methods for keeping time logs, such as digital tools, paper-based logs, and apps.

1.4 How to Keep a Time Log:

Provide step-by-step instructions on how to start and maintain a time log, including setting intervals and recording activities.

1.5 Consistency and Honesty:

Emphasize the importance of consistency and honesty when maintaining a time log to ensure accurate data.

Section 2: Analyzing Your Time Usage

2.1 Categorizing Activities:

Explain how to categorize recorded activities into meaningful groups, such as work-related, leisure, personal, and other categories.

2.2 Identifying Time Wasters:

Discuss the process of identifying activities that are not contributing to your goals and are, in fact, time-wasting.

2.3 Evaluating Time Allocation:

Provide guidance on assessing how much time you allocate to different areas of your life, such as work, family, and personal growth.

2.4 Goal Alignment:

Explore how to determine if your time usage aligns with your short-term and long-term goals.

2.5 Making Informed Changes:

Explain the process of using time analysis to make informed decisions about adjusting your daily routines and tasks.

Section 3: Benefits of Time Tracking and Analysis

3.1 Improved Time Management:

Discuss how time tracking and analysis can lead to better time management and increased productivity.

3.2 Stress Reduction:

Highlight how identifying time wasters and making changes can reduce stress and improve work-life balance.

3.3 Personal Growth:

Explain how analyzing your time can help you focus on personal growth and self-improvement.

Conclusion:

Keeping a time log and analyzing your time usage is a powerful practice for improving your time management skills and making more informed decisions about how to spend your time. By understanding how you currently allocate your time, you can make positive changes that align with your goals and priorities. In the next chapter, we will explore strategies for overcoming common time-related challenges and achieving greater work-life balance.

**Chapter 7: The Pomodoro Technique**

Introduction:

In a world filled with distractions and constant demands on our time, maintaining focus and productivity can be a challenge. In this chapter, we will explore the Pomodoro Technique, a time management method designed to enhance focus, productivity, and time management. By understanding and implementing the Pomodoro Technique, you can make significant improvements in your work habits.

Section 1: Explaining the Pomodoro Method

1.1 What is the Pomodoro Technique?

Define the Pomodoro Technique as a time management method developed by Francesco Cirillo, characterized by work intervals (Pomodoros) and short breaks.
1.2 The Pomodoro Timer:

Explain the use of a timer (typically set for 25 minutes) to mark the start of a Pomodoro and signal a break.
1.3 The Concept of Sprints:

Discuss how Pomodoros are used as focused work sprints, providing structured, uninterrupted periods of work.

1.4 Short Breaks:

Describe the purpose of short breaks (usually 5 minutes) between
Pomodoros and their role in maintaining productivity.

1.5 Long Breaks:

Explain the concept of longer breaks (15-30 minutes) after completing
a set of Pomodoros (typically four), allowing for rejuvenation.

Section 2: Implementing Pomodoro for Improved Focus

2.1 Setting Clear Goals:

Discuss the importance of setting clear and achievable goals before
starting a Pomodoro.

2.2 Eliminating Distractions:

Provide strategies for creating a distraction-free work environment
during Pomodoros.

2.3 Tracking Progress:

Explain how tracking your Pomodoros and tasks can help you evaluate
your productivity and make improvements.

2.4 Adjusting Work Intervals:

Discuss how to tailor the length of Pomodoros to your own attention
span and energy levels.

2.5 Combating Procrastination:

Highlight how the Pomodoro Technique can be effective in combating procrastination and enhancing motivation.

Section 3: Benefits of the Pomodoro Technique

3.1 Improved Concentration:

Explain how the structured work intervals of the Pomodoro Technique can boost concentration and minimize burnout.

3.2 Enhanced Productivity:

Discuss how Pomodoros can lead to increased productivity and task completion.

3.3 Time Management:

Explore how the Pomodoro Technique can improve time management by helping you allocate time effectively.

Conclusion:

The Pomodoro Technique is a valuable tool for enhancing focus, productivity, and time management. By implementing this method and making it a part of your daily work routine, you can experience improved concentration and efficiency. In the next chapter, we will explore additional strategies and tools for time management and personal growth.

**Chapter 8: Overcoming Procrastination**

Introduction:

Procrastination is a common challenge that can hinder productivity and personal growth. In this chapter, we will explore the root causes of procrastination and provide strategies to overcome this habit. By understanding the underlying factors and implementing effective techniques, you can conquer procrastination and accomplish your goals more efficiently.

Section 1: Understanding the Root Causes of Procrastination

1.1 Fear of Failure:

Discuss how the fear of failing or not meeting one's own standards can lead to procrastination.
1.2 Lack of Motivation:

Explain how a lack of motivation or interest in a task can result in avoidance and delay.
1.3 Perfectionism:

Explore how perfectionism, the desire for flawless results, can be a significant contributor to procrastination.
1.4 Task Difficulty:

Discuss how the perceived difficulty or complexity of a task can lead to avoidance and procrastination.

1.5 Lack of Self-Discipline:

Explain the role of self-discipline in task management and how its absence can lead to procrastination.

Section 2: Strategies to Overcome Procrastination

2.1 Goal Setting:

Discuss the importance of setting clear and achievable goals as a foundation for overcoming procrastination.

2.2 Prioritization:

Provide guidance on how to prioritize tasks and tackle the most important ones first.

2.3 Break Tasks into Smaller Steps:

Explain the benefits of breaking larger tasks into smaller, more manageable steps to reduce feelings of overwhelm.

2.4 Use of Time Management Techniques:

Explore the utilization of time management techniques like the Pomodoro Technique and task lists to enhance productivity.

2.5 Self-Motivation:

Discuss strategies for self-motivation, including finding intrinsic motivation, setting rewards, and eliminating distractions.

2.6 Challenge Negative Self-Talk:

Highlight the importance of recognizing and challenging negative self-talk and self-doubt that may contribute to procrastination.

Section 3: Benefits of Overcoming Procrastination

3.1 Increased Productivity:

Explain how overcoming procrastination can lead to increased productivity and task completion.

3.2 Reduced Stress:

Discuss how conquering procrastination can result in reduced stress and anxiety related to unfinished tasks.

3.3 Personal Growth:

Explore the potential for personal growth and development when procrastination is effectively managed.

Conclusion:

Procrastination can be a significant barrier to success, but by understanding its root causes and implementing effective strategies, you can overcome this habit and achieve your goals. In the next chapter, we will delve into techniques for effective time management and maintaining a healthy work-life balance.

**Chapter 9: Time Management Tools and Apps**

Introduction:

In the digital age, a wide array of time management tools and apps are available to help individuals streamline their productivity and manage their time effectively. In this chapter, we will review popular time management tools and explore strategies for selecting the right ones to suit your specific needs. By leveraging these tools, you can optimize your time management and improve your overall productivity.

Section 1: Review of Popular Time Management Tools

1.1 Task Management Apps:

Discuss the features and benefits of task management apps like Todoist, Wunderlist, and Trello.

1.2 Calendar Apps:

Explore calendar apps such as Google Calendar, Apple Calendar, and Microsoft Outlook, and how they can help you schedule and manage your time.

1.3 Note-Taking Apps:

Review popular note-taking apps like Evernote and OneNote, and their role in organizing information and tasks.

1.4 Time Tracking Software:

Discuss the purpose of time tracking software like Toggl and Clockify,

and how they can help you monitor your time usage.

1.5 Project Management Tools:

Examine project management tools like Asana and Basecamp and

their utility in managing complex tasks and projects.

Section 2: Selecting the Right Tools for Your Needs

2.1 Identify Your Needs:

Discuss the importance of identifying your specific time management

needs and goals before choosing a tool.

2.2 Consider Your Work Environment:

Explain how your work environment, whether it's in an office or remote,

can influence the choice of time management tools.

2.3 Compatibility and Integration:

Highlight the significance of selecting tools that are compatible with

your existing systems and can be seamlessly integrated.

2.4 Mobile Accessibility:

Discuss the importance of mobile accessibility, allowing you to manage

your tasks and time on the go.

2.5 User-Friendly Interfaces:

Emphasize the value of selecting tools with user-friendly interfaces that match your preferences and ease of use.
Section 3: Tips for Effective Implementation

3.1 Learning and Training:

Explain the importance of learning how to use your chosen time management tools effectively through training or self-guided learning.
3.2 Regular Updates and Maintenance:

Discuss the necessity of keeping your tools and apps updated and organized for optimal performance.
3.3 Integration with Your Workflow:

Provide guidance on how to integrate your chosen tools seamlessly into your daily workflow for maximum efficiency.
3.4 Flexibility and Adaptability:

Explore the benefits of being flexible and adaptable in using your time management tools, allowing for changes in your work style and goals.
Conclusion:

Time management tools and apps offer valuable support in managing your tasks and optimizing your productivity. By selecting the right tools that align with your needs and learning to use them effectively, you can enhance your time management skills and work more efficiently. In the next chapter, we will explore strategies for maintaining a work-life balance and avoiding burnout.

**Chapter 10: Planning and Scheduling**

Introduction:

Planning and scheduling are fundamental aspects of effective time management. In this chapter, we will explore the importance of daily, weekly, and monthly planning, as well as effective scheduling techniques. By developing a well-structured planning and scheduling system, you can maximize your productivity, achieve your goals, and maintain a healthy work-life balance.

Section 1: Daily Planning

1.1 The Daily To-Do List:

Discuss the role of a daily to-do list in structuring your tasks and ensuring you stay on track.

1.2 Prioritizing Daily Tasks:

Provide guidance on how to prioritize daily tasks, emphasizing the importance of completing critical tasks first.

1.3 Time Blocking:

Explain how time blocking can be used to allocate specific time slots for tasks and create a structured daily schedule.

1.4 Morning Routines:

Explore the concept of establishing morning routines to set a positive tone for the day and improve productivity.

Section 2: Weekly Planning

2.1 Weekly Goal Setting:

Discuss the process of setting weekly goals and how they should align with your longer-term objectives.

2.2 Reviewing the Past Week:

Highlight the importance of reviewing the previous week's accomplishments and areas for improvement.

2.3 Time Allocation:

Explain how to allocate your time across different tasks and projects throughout the week.

2.4 Weekly Planning Sessions:

Discuss the benefits of setting aside dedicated time for weekly planning sessions.

Section 3: Monthly Planning

3.1 Monthly Goal Setting:

Explore the practice of setting monthly goals that align with your long-term aspirations.

3.2 Monthly Calendars:

Discuss the use of monthly calendars to gain a holistic view of your commitments and deadlines.

3.3 Reflect and Adjust:

Explain how to use monthly planning to reflect on your progress and make necessary adjustments to your goals and priorities.

Section 4: Effective Scheduling Techniques

4.1 Time Blocking:

Reiterate the importance of time blocking, emphasizing how it can be applied not only to daily planning but also to weekly and monthly schedules.

4.2 Batch Processing:

Discuss the concept of batch processing, where similar tasks are grouped together to increase efficiency.

4.3 The Two-Minute Rule:

Explain the two-minute rule, which suggests that if a task can be completed in two minutes or less, it should be done immediately.

4.4 Schedule Buffer Time:

Highlight the value of including buffer time in your schedule to account for unexpected events and maintain flexibility.

Conclusion:

Effective planning and scheduling are essential skills for managing your time and achieving your goals. By implementing daily, weekly, and monthly planning practices and employing effective scheduling techniques, you can create a structured framework for your tasks and responsibilities, leading to increased productivity and a healthier work-life balance. In the next chapter, we will explore techniques for stress management and maintaining well-being in your time management journey.

**Chapter 11: Time Management in the Workplace**

Introduction:

Time management is crucial in the workplace to ensure productivity and efficiency. In this chapter, we will explore two essential aspects of time management in the workplace: meeting management and dealing with workplace distractions. By mastering these skills, you can make the most of your work hours and contribute to a more productive and focused work environment.

Section 1: Meeting Management

1.1 Meeting Effectiveness:

Discuss the importance of effective meetings and how they impact productivity and time management in the workplace.
1.2 Setting Clear Objectives:

Explain the significance of setting clear meeting objectives and agendas to keep discussions focused and efficient.
1.3 Time Allocation:

Provide guidance on allocating specific timeframes for meetings to avoid unnecessary delays.
1.4 Attendance and Participation:

Discuss the importance of inviting only essential participants and encouraging active participation during meetings.

1.5 Follow-Up and Action Items:

Highlight the necessity of documenting action items and follow-up plans to ensure that meetings lead to actionable outcomes.

Section 2: Dealing with Workplace Distractions

2.1 Identifying Common Distractions:

Discuss common workplace distractions, such as email, social media, and noisy environments.

2.2 Time-Blocking for Focus:

Explain the use of time-blocking techniques to allocate dedicated, distraction-free periods for focused work.

2.3 Digital Detox:

Explore the concept of a digital detox and its benefits in reducing the impact of technology-related distractions.

2.4 The Role of Breaks:

Discuss how strategically planned breaks can help refresh and refocus, mitigating the effects of workplace distractions.

2.5 Establishing Boundaries:

Provide strategies for setting boundaries in the workplace to minimize interruptions and distractions.

Section 3: Promoting a Productive Work Environment

3.1 Communication and Collaboration:

Explain the importance of effective communication and collaboration in reducing workplace distractions.

3.2 Clear Policies and Guidelines:

Discuss the role of clear workplace policies and guidelines for managing distractions and maintaining productivity.

3.3 Time Management Training:

Highlight the value of providing time management training to employees to enhance their productivity skills.

Conclusion:

Effective time management in the workplace is critical for both individual and organizational success. By mastering meeting management and dealing with workplace distractions, you can create a more focused and productive work environment. In the next chapter, we will explore strategies for stress management and maintaining well-being as you navigate the challenges of time management in both your personal and professional life.

**Chapter 12: Time Management for Students**

Introduction:

Time management is a vital skill for students, helping them excel academically while maintaining a balanced life. In this chapter, we will explore time management strategies tailored for students, focusing on effective study techniques and achieving a balance between academics and extracurricular activities.

Section 1: Study Techniques

1.1 Setting Clear Goals:

Explain the importance of setting clear academic goals, including exam preparation, assignment deadlines, and long-term objectives.

1.2 Active Learning:

Discuss active learning strategies, such as summarizing notes, asking questions, and participating in discussions, to enhance comprehension and retention.

1.3 Prioritizing Tasks:

Provide guidance on prioritizing assignments, readings, and study sessions based on their importance and deadlines.

1.4 Time-Blocking for Study:

Explain the use of time-blocking to allocate dedicated study periods, ensuring focused and uninterrupted study sessions.

1.5 Effective Note-Taking:

Discuss techniques for effective note-taking, including using keywords, summarizing information, and creating organized study materials.

Section 2: Balancing Academics and Extracurricular Activities

2.1 Time Allocation:

Discuss the importance of allocating time for both academic commitments and extracurricular activities, ensuring a balanced lifestyle.

2.2 Extracurricular Goals:

Explore the significance of setting goals for extracurricular involvement and aligning them with personal interests and long-term objectives.

2.3 Prioritization and Boundaries:

Provide strategies for prioritizing academic tasks and setting boundaries to avoid overcommitment in extracurricular activities.

2.4 Flexible Scheduling:

Explain how flexible scheduling can help accommodate academic requirements and extracurricular involvement.

2.5 Self-Care:

Highlight the importance of self-care, including proper sleep, nutrition, and relaxation, to maintain a healthy balance between academics and extracurriculars.

Section 3: Promoting a Supportive Learning Environment

3.1 Study Groups and Resources:

Discuss the benefits of study groups, academic resources, and peer support in enhancing academic performance.

3.2 Time Management Workshops:

Highlight the value of time management workshops and educational programs for students to develop effective time management skills.

3.3 Mentorship and Guidance:

Explain the role of mentors, teachers, and academic advisors in providing guidance and support to students.

Conclusion:

Time management for students is essential for academic success and personal well-being. By implementing effective study techniques, setting clear goals, and achieving a balance between academics and extracurricular activities, students can navigate their educational journey more efficiently. In the next chapter, we will explore stress

management techniques and strategies for maintaining overall
well-being while effectively managing your time.

**Chapter 13: Time Management for Parents**

Introduction:

Balancing the demands of family and work life is a significant challenge for parents. In this chapter, we will explore time management strategies tailored for parents, focusing on effectively juggling family and work responsibilities while ensuring quality time with children. By mastering these skills, parents can create a fulfilling and harmonious family life.

Section 1: Juggling Family and Work Responsibilities

1.1 Setting Clear Priorities:

Discuss the importance of establishing clear priorities between family and work responsibilities.

1.2 Effective Scheduling:

Explain the use of effective scheduling techniques to allocate dedicated time for both family and work commitments.

1.3 Communication and Collaboration:

Highlight the significance of open communication with your partner and effective collaboration in managing household and parenting duties.

1.4 Delegating and Outsourcing:

Provide strategies for delegating tasks and outsourcing when necessary to maintain a balanced family and work life.

1.5 Flexibility and Adaptability:

Explore the value of being flexible and adaptable in managing family and work responsibilities, especially in the face of unexpected events.

Section 2: Quality Time with Children

2.1 Creating Family Routines:

Discuss the benefits of creating consistent family routines that allow for quality time with children.

2.2 Active Engagement:

Explore the concept of active engagement with children, such as playtime, shared activities, and meaningful conversations.

2.3 Technology-Free Zones:

Explain the importance of designating technology-free zones and times to promote more meaningful interactions with children.

2.4 One-on-One Time:

Highlight the significance of spending one-on-one time with each child to strengthen the parent-child relationship.

2.5 Being Present:

Discuss the value of being fully present and attentive when interacting with your children, minimizing distractions from work or other responsibilities.

Section 3: Promoting a Supportive Family Environment

3.1 Co-Parenting and Support:

Explore the role of co-parenting and seeking support from extended family members or caregivers in maintaining a healthy family environment.

3.2 Time Management Strategies:

Share time management strategies with your partner to ensure both parents are aligned in managing family and work responsibilities.

3.3 Self-Care:

Emphasize the importance of self-care for parents to maintain physical and mental well-being, enabling them to better care for their children.

Conclusion:

Time management for parents is essential for creating a harmonious family life while fulfilling work responsibilities. By effectively juggling family and work commitments, setting clear priorities, and ensuring quality time with children, parents can foster strong family bonds and personal well-being. In the next chapter, we will explore strategies for stress management and maintaining overall well-being while effectively managing your time.

**Chapter 14: Time Management for Entrepreneurs**

Introduction:

Entrepreneurship is a demanding journey that often blurs the lines between business and personal life. In this chapter, we will explore time management strategies tailored for entrepreneurs, focusing on balancing business and personal life while avoiding burnout. By mastering these skills, entrepreneurs can achieve success while maintaining their well-being.

Section 1: Balancing Business and Personal Life

1.1 Defining Clear Boundaries:

Discuss the importance of setting clear boundaries between business and personal life to maintain a healthy balance.
1.2 Effective Scheduling:

Explain the use of effective scheduling techniques to allocate dedicated time for both business and personal commitments.
1.3 Delegating and Outsourcing:

Provide strategies for delegating tasks and outsourcing when necessary to prevent overextending yourself.
1.4 Time for Family and Relationships:

Highlight the significance of allocating time for family and nurturing
personal relationships outside of work.

1.5 Regular Breaks and Vacations:

Discuss the importance of regular breaks and vacations to recharge
and disconnect from work.

Section 2: Avoiding Burnout

2.1 Self-Care and Well-Being:

Explain the importance of self-care practices, including exercise,
relaxation, and stress management, to prevent burnout.

2.2 Time for Creativity and Innovation:

Discuss the value of allocating time for creativity and innovation within
your business to maintain enthusiasm.

2.3 Time Management Tools:

Explore the use of time management tools and techniques to
streamline work processes and reduce the risk of burnout.

2.4 Regular Assessment:

Provide guidance on regularly assessing your workload and
commitments to identify signs of burnout and make necessary
adjustments.

2.5 Seeking Support:

Highlight the significance of seeking support from mentors, peers, and professionals when experiencing burnout or overwhelming stress.

Section 3: Building a Supportive Business Environment

3.1 Team Collaboration:

Discuss the importance of fostering a collaborative and supportive team environment that can share the workload and responsibilities.

3.2 Effective Business Systems:

Emphasize the role of establishing efficient business systems and workflows that reduce the time and effort required for daily operations.

3.3 Business Strategy and Goals:

Explore how clear business strategies and goals can provide direction and focus, reducing the risk of overcommitment.

Conclusion:

Time management for entrepreneurs is essential for achieving business success while maintaining personal well-being. By balancing business and personal life, setting boundaries, and avoiding burnout through self-care and support, entrepreneurs can thrive in their ventures. In the next chapter, we will explore strategies for maintaining a work-life balance and overall well-being in your time management journey.

**Chapter 15: Delegating and Outsourcing**

Introduction:

Delegating and outsourcing are essential skills in effective time management, allowing you to focus on your core responsibilities and achieve greater productivity. In this chapter, we will explore the art of identifying tasks suitable for delegation and finding and managing outsourcing resources. By mastering these skills, you can streamline your workload and maximize your efficiency.

Section 1: Identifying Tasks to Delegate

1.1 Task Assessment:

Discuss the importance of assessing your tasks and responsibilities to identify which ones can be delegated.
1.2 Core vs. Non-Core Tasks:

Explain the concept of core tasks (those directly related to your main responsibilities) versus non-core tasks (supporting tasks that can be delegated).
1.3 Skills and Competencies:

Discuss how to evaluate your own skills and competencies to determine the tasks you excel in and those better suited for delegation.

1.4 Time Sensitivity:

Highlight the role of time sensitivity in deciding which tasks should be delegated, especially when facing tight deadlines.

1.5 Task Complexity:

Provide guidance on assessing the complexity of tasks and considering delegation for those that require specialized knowledge or expertise.

Section 2: Finding and Managing Outsourcing Resources

2.1 Identifying Suitable Outsourcing Partners:

Explain how to identify potential outsourcing partners, including freelancers, agencies, and contractors.

2.2 Quality and Reputation:

Discuss the importance of evaluating the quality and reputation of outsourcing resources, emphasizing the need for reliable and competent partners.

2.3 Communication and Expectations:

Explore the significance of clear communication and setting expectations when working with outsourcing partners.

2.4 Contracts and Agreements:

Highlight the value of formal contracts and agreements that outline the scope of work, deadlines, and payment terms.

2.5 Project Management and Oversight:

Provide strategies for effective project management and oversight when working with outsourcing partners to ensure successful collaboration.

Section 3: Benefits of Delegating and Outsourcing

3.1 Increased Productivity:

Explain how delegating and outsourcing can lead to increased productivity by allowing you to focus on core tasks.

3.2 Time Savings:

Discuss how these practices can save you valuable time that can be allocated to more important activities.

3.3 Specialized Expertise:

Highlight the benefits of gaining access to specialized expertise and skills through outsourcing.

3.4 Scalability:

Explore how delegating and outsourcing can make your operations more scalable and adaptable to changes in workload.

3.5 Work-Life Balance:

Emphasize how effective delegation and outsourcing can contribute to a healthier work-life balance by reducing your workload.

Conclusion:

Delegating and outsourcing are valuable tools in managing your time and responsibilities. By identifying tasks suitable for delegation and effectively finding and managing outsourcing resources, you can enhance your productivity and maintain a balanced work-life equilibrium. In the next chapter, we will explore strategies for maintaining overall well-being while managing your time effectively.

**Chapter 16: Time Management for Creatives**

Introduction:

Creativity often thrives on freedom and inspiration, but even the most imaginative individuals must manage their time effectively to balance creative pursuits with daily responsibilities. In this chapter, we will explore time management strategies tailored for creatives, focusing on achieving this balance and overcoming creative blocks. By mastering these skills, creative individuals can nurture their artistic endeavors while managing their commitments.

Section 1: Balancing Creative Pursuits with Daily Responsibilities

1.1 Identifying Your Peak Creative Times:

Discuss the importance of recognizing your most productive and creative times during the day.
1.2 Setting Boundaries:

Explain how setting boundaries can help you allocate time for creative work while also managing daily responsibilities.
1.3 Prioritizing Creative Tasks:

Provide guidance on how to prioritize creative projects and tasks to ensure they receive dedicated attention.

1.4 Time Blocking for Creativity:

Explore the use of time blocking techniques to allocate specific periods

for creative work, maintaining focus and discipline.

1.5 Flexible Scheduling:

Discuss the benefits of a flexible schedule that accommodates bursts

of creative inspiration, even within a structured routine.

Section 2: Creative Blocks and Overcoming Them

2.1 Recognizing Creative Blocks:

Explain common causes of creative blocks, such as self-doubt,

perfectionism, and burnout.

2.2 Freewriting and Brainstorming:

Highlight the value of freewriting and brainstorming techniques to

overcome creative blocks and stimulate fresh ideas.

2.3 Changing Perspectives:

Discuss how changing your perspective, environment, or medium can

help overcome creative stagnation.

2.4 Seeking Inspiration:

Explore how seeking inspiration from various sources, such as art,

nature, or other creatives, can rejuvenate your creativity.

2.5 Self-Care and Well-Being:

Emphasize the importance of self-care and maintaining well-being to

prevent burnout and maintain creativity.

Section 3: Promoting a Supportive Creative Environment

3.1 Collaborative Opportunities:

Discuss how collaborating with other creatives can provide a

supportive and inspiring environment for your work.

3.2 Feedback and Critique:

Explain the role of constructive feedback and critique in improving your

creative work.

3.3 Time Management Tools:

Explore the use of time management tools and techniques to

streamline your creative process and maintain your focus.

Conclusion:

Time management for creatives is crucial for nurturing your artistic

endeavors while managing daily responsibilities. By achieving a

balance between creative pursuits and routine tasks and developing

strategies to overcome creative blocks, you can enhance your

creativity and productivity. In the next chapter, we will explore stress management techniques and strategies for maintaining overall

well-being while effectively managing your time.

**Chapter 17: Time Management and Technology**

Introduction:

In our increasingly digital world, technology plays a significant role in both enabling productivity and presenting distractions. In this chapter, we will explore the relationship between time management and technology, focusing on managing digital distractions and leveraging technology for enhanced productivity. By mastering these skills, you can harness the power of technology to make the most of your time.

Section 1: Managing Digital Distractions

1.1 Identifying Digital Distractions:

Discuss common digital distractions, such as social media, emails, and notifications, and how they impact time management.

1.2 The Role of Mindfulness:

Explain how practicing mindfulness can help you become aware of digital distractions and their effect on your focus.

1.3 Digital Detox Strategies:

Provide techniques for implementing a digital detox, including setting specific boundaries and designated technology-free times.

1.4 App and Notification Management:

Explore how to manage apps and notifications on your devices to reduce interruptions and regain control of your time.

1.5 Effective Email Management:

Discuss strategies for efficient email management, including email batching, categorization, and setting response times.

Section 2: Leveraging Technology for Productivity

2.1 Time Management Apps:

Discuss the use of time management apps and tools to streamline your tasks and improve productivity.

2.2 Project Management Software:

Explore project management software and how it can enhance collaboration and task organization.

2.3 Automation and Workflows:

Explain the benefits of automating repetitive tasks and creating efficient workflows to save time.

2.4 Cloud-Based Collaboration:

Discuss the advantages of cloud-based collaboration tools for remote work and real-time information sharing.

2.5 Personal Assistant Technology:

Highlight the use of personal assistant technology, like voice-activated devices, to manage tasks and access information quickly.

Section 3: Striking a Balance

3.1 Setting Technology Boundaries:

Discuss the importance of setting clear boundaries with technology to avoid overuse and digital burnout.

3.2 Utilizing Technology Mindfully:

Explain the concept of mindful technology usage, which involves using technology with intention and awareness.

3.3 Regular Assessment:

Provide guidance on regularly assessing your technology habits and making adjustments to maintain a healthy balance.

Conclusion:

The relationship between time management and technology is multifaceted, with both challenges and opportunities. By effectively managing digital distractions and leveraging technology for productivity, you can make technology a valuable ally in your time management journey. In the next chapter, we will explore strategies for maintaining a work-life balance and overall well-being while effectively managing your time in our digital age.

**Chapter 18: Stress Reduction and Time Management**

Introduction:

The relationship between stress and time management is undeniable. Stress can be a significant barrier to effective time management, and poor time management can lead to increased stress. In this chapter, we will explore the connection between stress and time management and provide techniques for reducing stress while optimizing your time management skills. By mastering these strategies, you can lead a more balanced and productive life.

Section 1: The Connection Between Stress and Time Management

1.1 The Stress-Time Management Loop:

Discuss how poor time management can lead to increased stress, and, in turn, heightened stress can impair time management.
1.2 Impact of Procrastination:

Explain how procrastination, a common time management issue, can generate stress due to unmet deadlines and last-minute rushes.
1.3 Overcommitment and Burnout:

Highlight how overcommitment and excessive workload, often a result of poor time management, can lead to burnout and chronic stress.

1.4 Reduced Productivity:

Discuss how stress can diminish productivity and hinder efficient time
management.

1.5 Mindfulness and Self-Awareness:

Explore the importance of mindfulness and self-awareness in
recognizing the connection between stress and time management.

Section 2: Techniques for Stress Reduction

2.1 Time Management Techniques:

Provide time management strategies, such as prioritization, delegation,
and the Pomodoro Technique, to enhance productivity and reduce
stress.

2.2 Mindfulness and Meditation:

Explain how practicing mindfulness and meditation can reduce stress
by promoting relaxation and focus.

2.3 Stress-Reduction Activities:

Discuss stress-reduction activities like exercise, hobbies, and leisure
time, which can counteract the effects of stress.

2.4 Breathing Exercises:

Provide techniques for breathing exercises to manage stress and maintain composure in challenging situations.

2.5 Seeking Support:

Emphasize the importance of seeking support from friends, family, or professionals when dealing with high levels of stress.

Section 3: Achieving Balance

3.1 Prioritizing Well-Being:

Discuss the need to prioritize personal well-being, including physical and mental health, in achieving a balanced and stress-free life.

3.2 Setting Realistic Goals:

Explain the importance of setting achievable goals and boundaries to prevent overcommitment and reduce stress.

3.3 Regular Evaluation:

Provide guidance on regularly evaluating your time management strategies and stress levels to make necessary adjustments.

Conclusion:

The connection between stress and time management is a central aspect of personal productivity and well-being. By understanding this connection and implementing techniques for stress reduction, you can optimize your time management skills while maintaining a balanced and stress-free life. In the next chapter, we will explore strategies for maintaining a work-life balance and overall well-being as you navigate the challenges of time management in various aspects of your life.

**Chapter 19: Time Management for Better Health**

Introduction:

Maintaining good health is paramount for a fulfilling and productive life. In this chapter, we will explore the connection between time management and well-being, focusing on balancing work, exercise, and nutrition. We will also delve into the crucial role of sleep and its impact on effective time management. By mastering these strategies, you can lead a healthier and more balanced life.

Section 1: Balancing Work, Exercise, and Nutrition

1.1 Prioritizing Exercise:

Discuss the importance of prioritizing regular exercise to promote physical health and well-being.

1.2 Scheduling Workouts:

Provide guidance on scheduling workouts and integrating them into your daily or weekly routine.

1.3 Nutrition Planning:

Explain the significance of planning and maintaining a balanced diet for overall health and energy.

1.4 Meal Prep and Healthy Eating:

Discuss the benefits of meal preparation and making healthier eating choices, even during busy workdays.

1.5 Time-Blocking for Health:

Explore the use of time-blocking techniques to allocate dedicated time for exercise, meal planning, and self-care.

Section 2: Sleep and Its Impact on Time Management

2.1 The Importance of Sleep:

Highlight the crucial role of sleep in maintaining cognitive function, productivity, and overall health.

2.2 Sleep Hygiene:

Explain the concept of sleep hygiene and the practices that support quality sleep, including a regular sleep schedule and a conducive sleep environment.

2.3 The Connection Between Sleep and Productivity:

Discuss how inadequate sleep can hinder productivity and the effective management of time.

2.4 Power Naps:

Explore the benefits of power naps for a quick energy boost and increased alertness.

2.5 Balancing Sleep and Work:

Provide strategies for balancing work responsibilities with the need for adequate sleep to ensure optimal time management.

Section 3: Achieving Holistic Health and Balance

3.1 Stress Management:

Discuss the importance of stress management techniques in promoting overall health and time management.

3.2 Regular Health Check-Ups:

Explain the value of scheduling regular health check-ups to detect and address potential health issues.

3.3 Personal Well-Being:

Emphasize the need to prioritize personal well-being, including mental health and emotional balance.

Conclusion:

Balancing work, exercise, nutrition, and sleep is essential for better health and effective time management. By understanding the connection between time management and well-being and implementing strategies to prioritize your health, you can lead a more balanced and productive life. In the next chapter, we will explore the concept of work-life balance and its significance in managing your time effectively.

**Chapter 20: Time Management and Personal Finance**

Introduction:

Effective personal finance and time management go hand in hand. In this chapter, we will explore the connection between time management and financial well-being, focusing on budgeting and financial planning, as well as the strategic investment of time for financial growth. By mastering these skills, you can achieve greater financial stability and success.

Section 1: Budgeting and Financial Planning

1.1 Setting Financial Goals:

Discuss the importance of setting clear financial goals and how they relate to effective time management.

1.2 Creating a Budget:

Explain the process of creating a budget to track income, expenses, and savings, and how it helps manage finances efficiently.

1.3 Regular Financial Review:

Highlight the necessity of regular financial reviews to ensure that you stay on track with your financial goals.

1.4 Time Allocation for Financial Planning:

Provide guidance on allocating dedicated time for financial planning,
including bill payments, budget adjustments, and savings contributions.
1.5 Automation of Financial Tasks:

Explore the advantages of automating financial tasks, such as bill
payments and savings contributions, to save time and maintain
financial discipline.
Section 2: Investment of Time for Financial Growth

2.1 Financial Education:

Discuss the importance of investing time in financial education to make
informed decisions about investments, savings, and debt management.
2.2 Building Additional Income Streams:

Explain strategies for building additional income streams, such as side
businesses or investments, to enhance your financial growth.
2.3 Tax Planning:

Explore the role of time management in tax planning to maximize
savings through deductions and credits.
2.4 Long-Term Financial Planning:

Discuss the value of allocating time for long-term financial planning,
including retirement and estate planning.

2.5 Investment Strategies:

Provide insights into investment strategies and the importance of researching and monitoring investments to optimize returns.

Section 3: Achieving Financial Freedom and Balance

3.1 Financial Discipline:

Discuss the role of financial discipline in managing expenses, avoiding debt, and making the most of your resources.

3.2 Emergency Fund and Insurance:

Explain the significance of setting up an emergency fund and obtaining the appropriate insurance coverage to protect your financial stability.

3.3 Regular Financial Assessment:

Provide guidance on regularly assessing your financial health and making necessary adjustments to achieve financial balance.

Conclusion:

The relationship between time management and personal finance is a critical aspect of a successful and balanced life. By effectively managing your time for budgeting, financial planning, and investing, you can secure your financial future and maintain peace of mind. In the next chapter, we will explore the concept of work-life balance and its significance in managing your time effectively.

**Chapter 21: Long-Term Time Management Strategies**

Introduction:

Effective time management extends beyond daily tasks and short-term goals. In this chapter, we will explore long-term time management strategies that focus on setting meaningful goals and creating a life plan. By mastering these skills, you can navigate your life with purpose and direction, ensuring that your time is invested in activities that align with your aspirations.

Section 1: Setting Long-Term Goals

1.1 The Significance of Long-Term Goals:

Discuss the importance of setting long-term goals that provide a sense of purpose and direction.

1.2 SMART Goal Setting:

Explain the SMART (Specific, Measurable, Achievable, Relevant, Time-bound) criteria for setting effective long-term goals.

1.3 Prioritizing Goals:

Provide guidance on prioritizing long-term goals to ensure that they are aligned with your values and ambitions.

1.4 Goal Breakdown:

Discuss the process of breaking down long-term goals into smaller,

manageable milestones to track progress.

1.5 Goal Review and Adjustment:


Highlight the value of regularly reviewing and adjusting long-term goals

to adapt to changing circumstances.

Section 2: Creating a Life Plan


2.1 The Life Planning Process:


Explain the concept of life planning and the steps involved in creating a

comprehensive life plan.

2.2 Values and Priorities:


Discuss the role of personal values and priorities in shaping your life

plan and decision-making.

2.3 Career and Personal Aspirations:


Explore how your career and personal aspirations are integrated into

your life plan, providing clarity on your path.

2.4 Balancing Life Areas:


Provide guidance on balancing various life areas, including family,

career, health, and personal growth, within your life plan.

2.5 Review and Adaptation:

Emphasize the need to regularly review and adapt your life plan as you progress through different life stages and circumstances.

Section 3: Achieving Long-Term Success and Fulfillment

3.1 Consistency and Persistence:

Discuss the importance of consistency and persistence in working toward long-term goals and fulfilling your life plan.

3.2 Time Allocation for Long-Term Goals:

Explain how to allocate time in your daily, weekly, and monthly schedules for activities that align with your long-term goals.

3.3 Resilience and Adaptability:

Explore the qualities of resilience and adaptability in overcoming obstacles and unexpected challenges on your path.

3.4 Celebrating Milestones:

Discuss the significance of celebrating milestones and achievements along your journey to maintain motivation and a sense of accomplishment.

Conclusion:

Long-term time management strategies are the foundation for a purpose-driven and fulfilled life. By setting meaningful long-term goals, creating a life plan, and staying committed to your aspirations, you can make the most of your time and work towards a future that aligns with your values and ambitions. In the next chapter, we will recap the key principles of effective time management and provide a roadmap for your continued success.

**Chapter 22: Handling Time Management Challenges**

Introduction:

Time management, while highly beneficial, is not without its challenges. In this chapter, we will explore strategies for handling setbacks and obstacles in your time management journey. We will also delve into the concept of building resilience, which is essential for maintaining your progress in the face of adversity.

Section 1: Handling Setbacks and Obstacles

1.1 Recognizing Common Setbacks:

Discuss common setbacks and obstacles that individuals encounter in their time management efforts, such as unexpected events, procrastination, or overcommitment.

1.2 Problem Solving and Adaptation:

Provide guidance on problem-solving strategies and adapting to unforeseen circumstances to minimize the impact of setbacks.

1.3 Time Management Assessment:

Discuss the importance of regular time management assessments to identify areas where challenges frequently arise.

1.4 Seeking Support:

Highlight the value of seeking support from mentors, peers, or professionals when facing persistent time management challenges.

1.5 Mindset and Perspective:

Explore how a positive mindset and a resilient perspective can help you approach setbacks as opportunities for growth.

Section 2: Building Resilience

2.1 Understanding Resilience:

Define resilience and explain how it relates to your ability to bounce back from adversity in your time management journey.

2.2 Emotional Regulation:

Discuss the importance of emotional regulation in maintaining a resilient outlook and managing stress.

2.3 Self-Confidence and Self-Efficacy:

Explore how self-confidence and self-efficacy contribute to resilience and the belief that you can overcome challenges.

2.4 Support Networks:

Explain the role of support networks, including friends, family, and mentors, in building resilience by providing encouragement and guidance.

2.5 Self-Care and Well-Being:

Emphasize the significance of self-care and well-being practices in nurturing resilience and maintaining a healthy mindset.

Section 3: Maintaining Progress

3.1 Learning from Challenges:

Discuss how setbacks and obstacles can be valuable learning experiences that contribute to your growth in time management.

3.2 Flexibility and Adaptability:

Provide strategies for remaining flexible and adaptable in your time management approach, allowing you to navigate challenges more effectively.

3.3 Setting Realistic Expectations:

Explain how setting realistic expectations and goals can prevent the undue pressure that may lead to setbacks.

3.4 Self-Reflection:

Highlight the importance of self-reflection in assessing your time management journey and making continuous improvements.

Conclusion:

Handling time management challenges and building resilience are essential components of a successful time management strategy. By learning to navigate setbacks, staying resilient in the face of adversity, and maintaining a mindset of growth, you can overcome obstacles and continue to improve your time management skills. In the final chapter, we will recap the key principles of effective time management and offer guidance for your continued success.

**Chapter 23: Maintaining Work-Life Balance**

Introduction:

Work-life balance is a crucial component of effective time management and overall well-being. In this chapter, we will explore strategies for achieving and maintaining a balanced life, as well as the importance of reevaluating priorities regularly. By mastering these skills, you can lead a fulfilling life that harmonizes your personal and professional responsibilities.

Section 1: Strategies for Achieving a Balanced Life

1.1 Prioritization of Time:

Discuss the significance of setting clear priorities in your life to allocate time effectively to different areas.

1.2 Time Management Techniques:

Provide guidance on utilizing time management techniques, such as setting boundaries, delegation, and effective scheduling, to balance work and personal life.

1.3 Flexible Scheduling:

Explain the advantages of a flexible schedule that allows for adjustments as needed to balance work and personal commitments.

1.4 Quality Over Quantity:

Discuss the importance of valuing the quality of time spent in both work and personal life over sheer quantity.

1.5 Setting Boundaries:

Explore the concept of setting boundaries to protect personal time and prevent work from encroaching on your personal life.

Section 2: Reevaluating Priorities

2.1 Regular Assessment:

Explain the importance of regularly assessing your priorities and evaluating whether they still align with your long-term goals and values.

2.2 Adapting to Life Changes:

Discuss how major life changes, such as career transitions, family growth, or personal development, may require a reevaluation of your priorities.

2.3 Delegating and Outsourcing:

Highlight the role of delegating tasks and outsourcing responsibilities to adjust your time allocation based on shifting priorities.

2.4 Self-Reflection:

Emphasize the value of self-reflection in understanding your evolving needs and ensuring that your priorities remain aligned with your values.

2.5 Seeking Support:

Explore how seeking support from friends, family, or mentors can provide guidance and assistance during periods of reevaluation.

Section 3: Achieving Long-Term Balance

3.1 Consistency and Adaptability:

Discuss the need for a consistent approach to work-life balance, while also recognizing the importance of adaptability when circumstances change.

3.2 Setting Realistic Expectations:

Explain how setting realistic expectations for your work and personal life can help you maintain balance and reduce stress.

3.3 Celebration and Self-Care:

Highlight the importance of celebrating achievements and engaging in self-care practices to maintain your well-being during your journey.

Conclusion:

Maintaining work-life balance is essential for leading a fulfilling and harmonious life. By implementing strategies for achieving a balanced life, reevaluating priorities, and remaining adaptable, you can continue to thrive while managing your time effectively. In the final chapter, we will recap the key principles of effective time management and offer guidance for your continued success and well-being.

**Chapter 24: Measuring Your Progress**

Introduction:

Measuring your progress is a fundamental aspect of effective time management. In this chapter, we will explore techniques for tracking your time management improvements and making necessary adjustments to your strategies. By mastering these skills, you can continually enhance your time management abilities and lead a more productive and balanced life.

Section 1: Tracking Your Time Management Improvements

1.1 Goal-Tracking Systems:

Discuss the use of goal-tracking systems to monitor your progress in achieving both short-term and long-term time management goals.

1.2 Time Logs and Journals:

Explain how maintaining time logs and journals can provide insight into how you allocate your time and help identify areas for improvement.

1.3 Performance Metrics:

Explore the importance of defining key performance metrics related to your time management goals and regularly assessing your performance against them.

1.4 Feedback and Self-Assessment:

Highlight the value of seeking feedback from peers, mentors, or using self-assessment to gain a comprehensive view of your time management improvements.

1.5 Data Analysis:

Discuss the role of data analysis in identifying patterns and trends in your time management practices, which can inform adjustments.

Section 2: Adjusting Your Strategies

2.1 Identifying Inefficiencies:

Provide guidance on recognizing inefficiencies and time-wasting behaviors in your daily routines, based on the data and feedback you've collected.

2.2 Refining Time Management Techniques:

Explain how to refine and adapt your time management techniques based on the data and insights you've gathered.

2.3 Delegation and Outsourcing:

Discuss the role of delegation and outsourcing in optimizing your time management by offloading non-core tasks.

2.4 Goal Modification:

Explore the concept of modifying your goals and priorities when circumstances or your objectives change.

2.5 Continuous Learning:

Emphasize the importance of continuous learning and self-improvement in refining your time management strategies.

Section 3: Sustaining Progress

3.1 Consistency:

Discuss the value of consistency in maintaining the progress you've achieved in your time management journey.

3.2 Accountability and Support:

Explain how accountability systems and support networks can help you stay on track and sustain your progress.

3.3 Celebrating Achievements:

Highlight the significance of celebrating your achievements and milestones to maintain motivation and positivity.

Conclusion:

Measuring your progress and making necessary adjustments are vital components of effective time management. By implementing tracking methods, analyzing your data, and remaining adaptable, you can continually refine your time management strategies and lead a more productive and balanced life. In the final chapter, we will recap the key principles of effective time management and offer guidance for your continued success and well-being.

**Chapter 25: Conclusion and Action Plan**

Introduction:

In this final chapter, we will summarize the key takeaways from this comprehensive guide on time management. After reflecting on the principles and strategies discussed throughout the book, you will be guided in developing a personalized time management action plan. This plan will help you apply what you've learned and embark on a journey towards more productive, fulfilling, and balanced living.

Section 1: Summarizing Key Takeaways

1.1 Time is a Precious Resource:

Emphasize the importance of recognizing time as a finite and valuable resource that should be managed effectively.

1.2 Setting Clear Goals:

Highlight the role of setting clear, specific, and achievable goals as the foundation of effective time management.

1.3 Prioritization is Key:

Explain the significance of prioritization in focusing on what matters most and avoiding time-wasting activities.

1.4 Time Management Techniques:

Discuss a variety of time management techniques, including the Pomodoro Technique, Eisenhower's Matrix, and task delegation.

1.5 Work-Life Balance:

Emphasize the importance of achieving a balance between work and personal life to maintain well-being and fulfillment.

Section 2: Developing Your Time Management Action Plan

2.1 Self-Assessment:

Encourage self-assessment to identify your current time management strengths and weaknesses.

2.2 Goal Setting:

Guide you in setting clear short-term and long-term time management goals that align with your values and aspirations.

2.3 Strategy Selection:

Help you select specific time management strategies from this book that resonate with your goals and areas of improvement.

2.4 Implementation Plan:

Provide a framework for developing a detailed plan for integrating these strategies into your daily, weekly, and monthly routines.

2.5 Accountability and Evaluation:

Suggest setting up accountability mechanisms and regular evaluations to track your progress and make necessary adjustments.

Section 3: Your Time Management Journey

3.1 Consistency:

Stress the importance of consistency in applying time management principles and maintaining progress.

3.2 Flexibility and Adaptability:

Remind you to remain flexible and adaptable, as your goals and circumstances may evolve over time.

3.3 Celebrating Achievements:

Highlight the significance of celebrating your achievements and milestones along your time management journey.

Conclusion:

In conclusion, effective time management is a journey that begins with awareness and is sustained through consistent effort. By reflecting on the key takeaways from this book and developing a personalized action plan, you can take the first steps towards a more productive, fulfilling, and balanced life. We hope this guide has been valuable to you, and we wish you success in your ongoing time management journey.